CRAFTS FROM MANY CULTURES

PUPPETS

Meryl Doney

Gareth Stevens Publishing
A WORLD ALMANAC EDUCATION GROUP COMPANY

About this Book

In this book you will find examples of puppets from a wide variety of countries and backgrounds. The puppet theater of each country has its own distinctive style, with different designs, colors, and traditions. Maps show you where each type of puppet comes from. Each left-hand page describes a puppet from one or more countries. Full-color photographs show puppets that have been made by native craftspeople. Each right-hand page provides step-by-step instructions, with illustrations, for making a puppet. As you go along, freely adapt ideas from this book and invent your own puppet characters.

When you decorate your puppets, the theater, and props, use traditional designs or patterns copied from other books on the country your puppets come from. By using those designs, you will make your theater look more like the real thing.

Most of the steps for making the projects in this book are easy to follow, but wherever you see this symbol, ask for help from an adult.

Measurement Conversions:

1 inch = 2.54 centimeters (cm)
1 yard = 0.9144 meters

Please visit our web site at: www.garethstevens.com
For a free color catalog describing Gareth Stevens Publishing's list of high-quality books and multimedia programs, call 1-800-542-2595 (USA) or 1-800-387-3178 (Canada). Gareth Stevens Publishing's fax: (414) 332-3567.

Library of Congress Cataloging-in-Publication Data

Doney, Meryl, 1942-
    Puppets / by Meryl Doney.
        p. cm. — (Crafts from many cultures)
    Includes bibliographical references and index.
    Contents: Puppet history — Dancing puppets — Poland and India — Hand puppets — China — Papier-mâché glove puppets — Britain — Carved wooden puppets — Mali and Tunisia — Shadow puppets — Indonesia — Comic shadow puppets — Greece and Turkey — Rod puppets — Indonesia — Lifelike puppets — Japan — String puppets — India — Marionettes — Burma — Animal string puppets — India — Putting on a play.
    ISBN 0-8368-4047-X (lib. bdg.)
    1. Puppet making—Juvenile literature. 2. Puppets—Juvenile literature. [1. Puppet making. 2. Puppets. 3. Handicraft.] I. Title.
TT174.7.D66 2004
745.592'24—dc22   2003060567

This North American edition first published in 2004 by
Gareth Stevens Publishing
A World Almanac Education Group Company
330 West Olive Street, Suite 100
Milwaukee, Wisconsin 53212 USA

This U.S. edition copyright © 2004 by Gareth Stevens, Inc.
Original edition copyright © 1995 by Franklin Watts.
Text © 1995 by Meryl Doney.

First published as *World Crafts: Puppets* in 1995 by Franklin Watts, 96 Leonard Street, London WC2A 4XD, England. Additional end matter copyright © 2004 by Gareth Stevens, Inc.

Franklin Watts series editor: Annabel Martin
Franklin Watts editor: Jane Walker
Design: Visual Image
Artwork: Ruth Levy
Photography: Peter Millard

Additional photographs:
C. Bowman/Robert Harding Picture Library: 10; Japan National Tourist Office, London: 20.

Gareth Stevens editor: Jonny Brown
Gareth Stevens cover design: Kami Koenig

Very special thanks to Alison Croft, educational advisor and puppet maker.

Printed in the United States of America

1 2 3 4 5 6 7 8 9 08 07 06 05 04

Contents

Puppet History

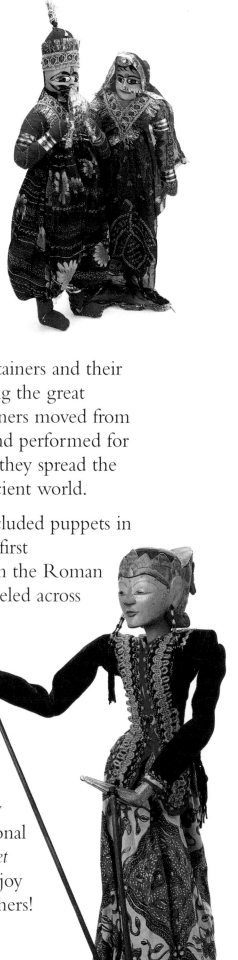

Traditional puppet theaters exist in almost every country in the world. One of the earliest puppets, a monkey character, was discovered in India and may be over four thousand years old. There are also early records of plays about legendary heroes and gods being acted by shadow, rod, and marionette puppets in China and the Far East.

From these early beginnings in Asia, entertainers and their puppets probably traveled along the great trading routes. As the entertainers moved from place to place, they stopped and performed for the local people. In this way, they spread the art of puppetry across the ancient world.

The Greeks and Romans included puppets in their religious plays, and the first Christians used them to teach Bible stories. When the Roman Empire fell apart, actors and puppeteers again traveled across Europe entertaining everyone from kings to the crowds in the marketplace.

Puppets were brought to North America and Australia in the 1800s by emigrants from Europe. There is evidence, however, that the North American Indians and Aboriginal peoples of Australia had puppet traditions before then.

Today, puppets are more popular than ever. Many famous characters have been created for international TV programs such as *Sesame Street* and *The Muppet Show* as well as for feature films. We hope you enjoy making your puppets and performing plays for others!

Your Own Puppet-Making Kit

As you begin making your puppets, look around for scraps of fabric, buttons, cardboard tubes, and yogurt cups. Keep these items in a box with a set of tools ready for making puppets.

Make some dough from the recipes below and store that, too. Wrap it in plastic wrap and keep it in a container with a tight lid.

Here are some useful items for your puppet-making kit:

hammer ▪ back saw ▪ hacksaw ▪ awl ▪ hand drill ▪ needle-nosed pliers ▪ scissors ▪ craft knife ▪ staple gun ▪ metal ruler ▪ brushes ▪ white acrylic paint ▪ poster paints ▪ varnish ▪ PVA (wood) glue ▪ strong glue ▪ modeling clay ▪ clear tape ▪ masking tape ▪ cardboard ▪ paper ▪ tissue

paper ▪ newspaper ▪ pen ▪ pencil ▪ felt-tipped pens ▪ fabric and felt ▪ needle and thread ▪ decorations, such as sequins, braid, aluminum foil, sticky shapes, beads ▪ newspaper to work on ▪ cardboard to cut on ▪ apron ▪ paper towels for cleaning up

Potato Dough

This no-bake recipe comes from Peru. It is made from mashed potatoes and plaster of paris. You will need the following:

3 tablespoons instant mashed potato flakes
10 tablespoons of plaster of paris water

In a small bowl, mix the potato flakes with 5 ounces of boiling water. Beat with a fork until fluffy.

In a larger bowl, mix the plaster of paris with 3 tablespoons of cold water. Stir it with a spoon until smooth.

Combine the two mixtures and knead well to blend them completely.

Salt Dough

2 cups of flour
$\frac{1}{2}$ cup of salt
$\frac{3}{4}$ cup of water

Mix the flour and salt together in a large bowl.

Make a well in the middle of the flour and salt mixture, add a little water, and stir with a fork. Continue adding small amounts of water, stirring each time, until all of the water is gone.

Finish mixing and kneading the dough with your hands. If the dough is too sticky, add more flour; if it is too dry, add more water.

Salt dough must be dried in an oven to make it harden.

Dancing Puppets

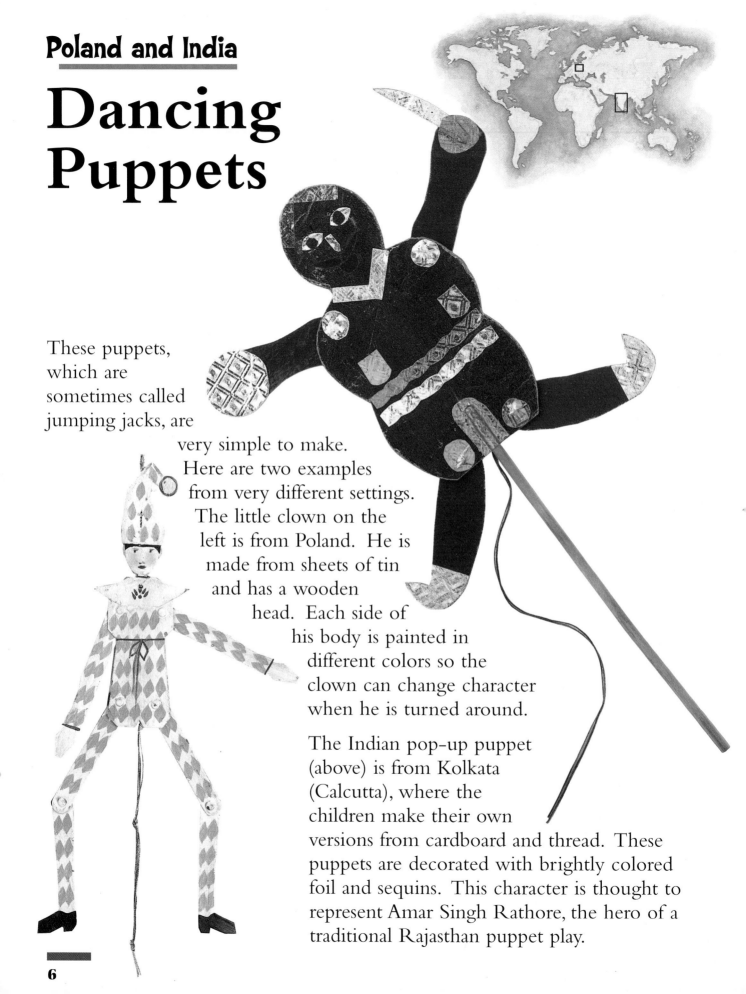

These puppets, which are sometimes called jumping jacks, are very simple to make. Here are two examples from very different settings. The little clown on the left is from Poland. He is made from sheets of tin and has a wooden head. Each side of his body is painted in different colors so the clown can change character when he is turned around.

The Indian pop-up puppet (above) is from Kolkata (Calcutta), where the children make their own versions from cardboard and thread. These puppets are decorated with brightly colored foil and sequins. This character is thought to represent Amar Singh Rathore, the hero of a traditional Rajasthan puppet play.

Make an Indian Pop-Up Puppet

You will need: cardboard ▪ glue ▪ foil ▪ colored paper ▪ needle ▪ thread ▪ plant stick ▪ clear tape

1 Cut simple body parts from cardboard. Glue on pieces of aluminum foil and colored paper to make the face and uniform. Cover the shield and saber with foil. Make two small holes in the top of each arm and leg. Make four holes in the body as shown.

2 Using the holes that are nearest the edges, join the arms together with thread. Knot the thread at the back. Join the legs in the same way.

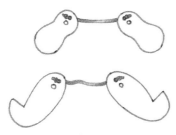

3 Attach the arms to the body with thread using the other holes on the arms. Knot the thread at the back and front. Attach the legs in the same way.

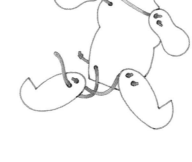

4 Use another thread to join the arms and legs, so you can make the puppet jump.

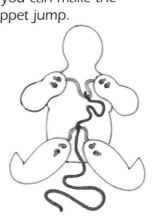

Cover the back by gluing a piece of colored paper onto the back of the neck.

5 Split the top .75 inch of a small, green plant stick. Push the puppet into it and secure the joint with tape. (You can tidy up the split end and knots by covering them with foil.) Attach the shield and saber.

Hand Puppets

China has a history of puppet-making that goes back over 2,000 years. This glove puppet is based on the historic Ku Li Tzu puppet theater. The puppeteer carried his puppets from town to town in a small box-like theater slung from the end of a pole. To begin the show, he would prop the pole against a wall and unroll curtains from below the stage to hide himself. After the show he would hoist the whole thing onto his shoulder again and move on to the next village.

Like the characters in Chinese opera, this puppet's face is painted to show his personality. He is a young man with no beard. You could make your puppet angry or sad, young or old.

Make a Ku Li Tzu Puppet

You will need: salt dough (see recipe, page 5) ▪ a cork ▪ paints ▪ varnish ▪ cardboard ▪ PVA glue ▪ colored fabric ▪ white or beige fabric ▪ ribbon ▪ felt pen ▪ rice (uncooked)

1 To make the head, use a piece of dough about 1 inch around. Push a cork into it and mold more dough around the cork to form the neck. Model the chin and add small pieces of dough for the facial features.

2 For boots, roll two small sausage shapes. Bend them into L-shapes, flatten the soles and point the toes. Model two smaller pieces of dough into hands. Bake the dough shapes at 300° Fahrenheit (150° Centigrade) until hard (about 40 minutes). Remove the cork and allow the head to cool in the oven.

3 Paint the pieces white, and add color. Varnish.

4 Cut out four pieces of cardboard for the headdress. Glue the rectangle around the head, fold in the sides, and staple at the top. Glue on the other pieces of cardboard and decorate.

front

back

5 Cut out two pieces of fabric for the robe. Pin and sew them, right sides together, leaving arm and neck holes. Hem. Glue the head and hands into the holes. Turn the robe right side out. Decorate it and add ribbon trim to the neck.

6 Cut out the front panel and hem it. Decorate it with felt pen. Sew it to the front of the robe. Make legs from two rectangles of white fabric. Sew up the sides to make tubes. Turn the legs right side out. Glue a boot into each tube. Fill the legs with rice, leaving 1.5 inches empty at the top.

7 Fold in .5 inch of fabric at the top of the legs. Then pin the legs inside the front of the robe under the panel. Sew them in place.

Sewing hint: To make a strong seam, sew one way with a running stitch, and then come back again filling in the spaces.

Papier-Mâché Glove Puppets

Mr. Punch, as we know him today, is a puppet with a fascinating history. As far as we can discover, he began life in Italy as a funny character called Pulcinello. Italian puppets were based on *commedia dell'arte*, a popular type of drama in which several clowns, or *zanni*, kept the people laughing. Pulcinello was a little man with a very hooked nose and chin and a hunched back. He wore a ruff around his neck and a pointed hat with a bell.

Mr. Punch was brought to England in about 1660. At that time he was a marionette, not a glove puppet. The English loved puppet plays because they often poked fun at the authorities. By 1825, puppet stories about Mr. Punch and his wife, Joan (her name later changed to Judy), had become favorites.

Make Mr. Punch

Traditional Punch characters were carved from wood, but this one has a papier-mâché head and a fabric body. The head is quite big compared to the body, but it must be light so your hand can move the puppet easily.

To perform a traditional play, you will also need to make Judy, her baby, the policeman, and the crocodile.

You will need: newspaper ▪ piece of stiff cardboard ▪ masking tape ▪ light cardboard ▪ toothpick ▪ modeling clay ▪ PVA glue ▪ cotton balls or batting ▪ paints ▪ varnish ▪ fabric ▪ felt ▪ rickrack ▪ a bell

1 Scrunch paper into a head shape, and stick it onto the stiff cardboard with masking tape. Roll a piece of light cardboard around your finger, and tape it to form a tube. Push the tube under the paper to make the neck.

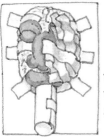

2 Push a shortened toothpick into the head where you want to attach a nose. Be sure it sticks out a little. Form the nose out of modeling clay and press it onto the toothpick. Add eyebrows, eyes, and a mouth. Add papier-mâché by sticking small pieces of newspaper, in layers, over the face.

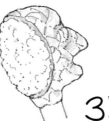

3 When dry, cut the head away from the cardboard. Fill the back with cotton. Cut out two cardboard ears, and stick them to the head with tape. Cover the back of the head with more papier-mâché and leave it to harden. Paint it with white acrylic before painting features with colored paints. Varnish.

4 To dress Mr. Punch, fold a piece of fabric in two and cut two pieces for the body. Pin and sew them, leaving the neck and bottom edge open. Turn the body right side out, and hem it. Sew a running stitch along the edge of a strip of felt to make a drawstring for the ruff.

5 Measure halfway around the head and make a three-piece pattern for the hat. Cut the pieces from felt, and sew them. Decorate the clothes with rickrack. Cut out four hand shapes from felt.

6 Glue the neck of the body to the head tube. Tie on the ruff with the drawstring. Glue the hat and brim to the head. Glue the hands together, leaving the cuffs open. Glue the hands to the arms. Add a bell to his hat!

Carved Wooden Puppets

At first, these African figures often seem very different from most other puppets. They have few moving parts and are more like carved figures. They are genuine puppets, however, and are used by storytellers to teach history, to tell legendary tales, and to pass on the values of the tribe or village group.

The woman puppet on the left is a Marka marionette from Tenne in Mali. The Marka, who are part of the Senoufo tribe, use puppets to tell traditional fables. This one is carved from one piece of wood. Her face and head are decorated with strips of tin. Her arms move when a string is pulled from below. The warrior on the right, with his shield and scimitar, is from Tunisia, North Africa. He may be the same character as the Indian dancing puppet on page 6. If so, he has traveled to North Africa from India. Puppet characters often moved from country to country as entertainers traveled. The warrior has no strings. The storyteller would probably hold him in his hand and act out the story.

Make an African Warrior

You will need: balsa wood for the body, hands, and legs, one piece 2.5 x 2.5 x 16 inches, two pieces 1 x 1 x 2 inches, and two pieces 1 x 1 x 18 inches ▪ PVA glue ▪ paints ▪ varnish ▪ knitting needle ▪ piece of wire ▪ two washers or buttons ▪ large sheet of gold cardboard ▪ 18 x 16-inch piece of fabric for the skirt ▪ two pieces of 5.5 x 11-inch fabric for the arms

1 Mark the puppet's features on the largest piece of wood, using one corner as his nose. Grip the wood in a vise.

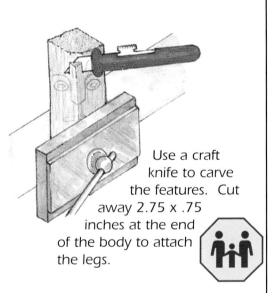

Use a craft knife to carve the features. Cut away 2.75 x .75 inches at the end of the body to attach the legs.

2 For feet, cut a 2-inch piece off the end of each leg. Glue the feet to the legs at right angles. Cut a piece .5 x 2.5 inches from the top of each leg. Use the craft knife to cut out a wrist shape at one end of each hand. Cut V shapes for fingers. Paint all pieces white and then apply poster paints. Varnish.

3 Use a knitting needle to make holes through the legs and body. Thread a piece of wire through the first leg, a washer, the body, a washer, and the other leg. Twist the ends so the legs are secure but can move freely.

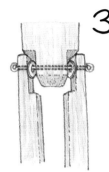

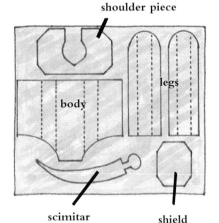

shoulder piece

body

legs

scimitar

shield

4 Draw the pieces of armor on gold cardboard. Cut them out. Decorate the armor by scoring and denting it with a blunt pencil.

5 Sew the sides of the skirt together and hem it. Sew a running stitch around the top and pull it to gather the waist. Sew down one side of each arm piece, right sides together. Turn the arms right side out. Iron them flat. Staple the hands to the arms.

6 Staple the dress to the waist and the arms to the shoulders. Wrap armor around the body. Add the shoulder piece and staple it to the back. Staple armor to the legs, the shield to one hand, and the scimitar to the other.

Shadow Puppets

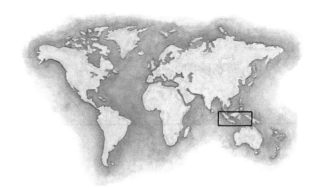

The fascinating art of the shadow puppet may have begun in Southeast Asia. Today the tradition of these puppets remains strong in Indonesia, China, and India.

Originally, shadow puppets represented people's ancestors, whose spirits were invited to enter the puppets. The spirits gave messages and advice on family matters or in times of danger. Today the plays are usually seen as entertainments or as ways of teaching people, but the performances still seem almost magical.

In a typical shadow theater, the puppets are held against a white screen that is tightly stretched across a wooden frame.

The performance begins in the evening, lit from behind by an oil lamp, and can go on all night. The puppet master must be a man of many talents. He operates the puppets, tells the story, directs the orchestra, and sometimes plays a musical instrument as well!

This is a Wayang Kulit puppet from Java. "*Wayang*" means "shadow," and "*kulit*" means "skin" or "leather."

Make a Wayang Kulit Puppet

You will need: cereal-box cardboard ▪ gold poster paint ▪ paints ▪ varnish ▪ modeling clay ▪ a needle ▪ split brass fasteners ▪ three green plant sticks

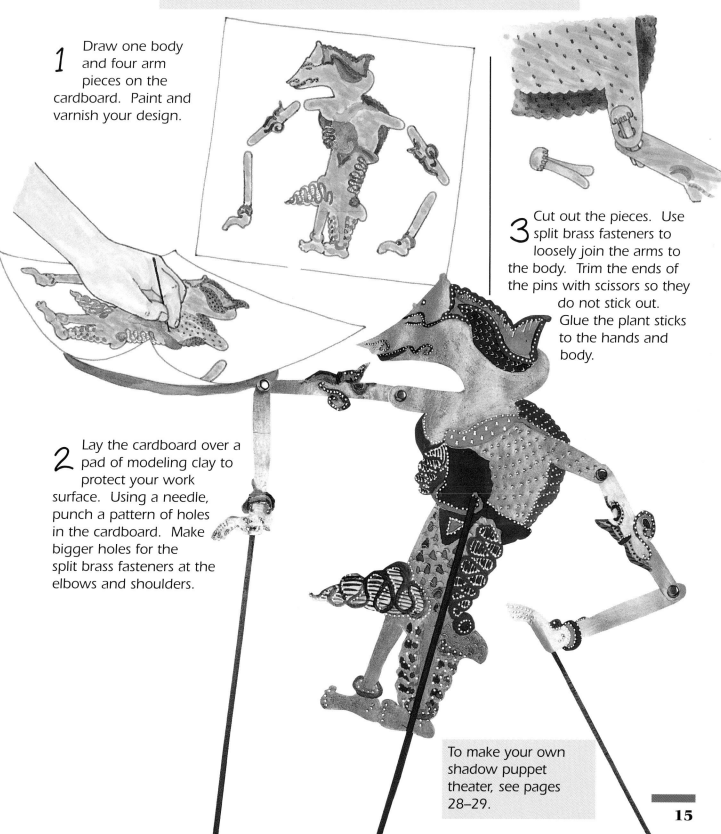

1 Draw one body and four arm pieces on the cardboard. Paint and varnish your design.

2 Lay the cardboard over a pad of modeling clay to protect your work surface. Using a needle, punch a pattern of holes in the cardboard. Make bigger holes for the split brass fasteners at the elbows and shoulders.

3 Cut out the pieces. Use split brass fasteners to loosely join the arms to the body. Trim the ends of the pins with scissors so they do not stick out. Glue the plant sticks to the hands and body.

To make your own shadow puppet theater, see pages 28–29.

Comic Shadow Puppets

Karagöz

No one knows exactly how the tradition of shadow puppets came to Europe. They may have traveled from the Far East via India or Arabia. These characters from Greece and Turkey are a mixture of the *wayang* tradition of Asia (page 14) and Mr. Punch of Europe (page 10). Karagöz is the hero from the Turkish shadow puppet theater. He and his friend Hacivat are rough, funny characters who enjoy slapstick fun and fighting. They are also greedy and love food. The plays are performed against a screen, with an olive-oil lamp providing the lighting. The colors show through the screen and look like stained glass. Karagöz is operated with one or two sticks, so he can fight, fall over, and even do a somersault with a deft twist of the puppeteer's wrist. The stories in Greek shadow puppet theater come from Turkey. Greek puppet plays feature the same characters, but they are called Karagiosis and Haziavadis.

Karagiosis

Make Karagöz, the Turkish Hero

Make sure that Karagöz and Hacivat face in opposite directions so that they can talk to each other on stage.

Adapt the method described here to make other characters for your plays.

You will need: white cardboard ▪ felt-tipped pens ▪ cooking oil ▪ modeling clay ▪ split brass fasteners ▪ two .25-inch dowel rods, 12 inches long ▪ thumbtacks

3 Attach the rods to the puppet by pushing a thumbtack through the card and into the end of each dowel. To store the puppets, remove the rods and place the puppets in a plastic bag to keep the oil from drying out.

Hacivat

1 Draw each puppet piece faintly on cardboard. Color them with felt-tipped pens. Rub cooking oil into both sides of the cardboard to make it transparent.

2 Cut out the pieces. Make joining holes by pushing a pencil through the cardboard and into a piece of modeling clay. Use split brass fasteners to loosely join the pieces together.

Rod Puppets

Rod puppets are made from carved wood. The head is mounted on a long rod that passes through the body. The puppeteer moves the head by twisting this rod with one hand while moving the arms with two rods held in the other hand. Rod puppets have long skirts instead of legs.

The puppet below comes from the Wayang Purwa plays, which tell traditional Hindu stories. Good and bad characters can be distinguished by the way they look. Even the angle of a puppet's head can be important. The puppet on the right is from Java. She is a character from the Wayang Golek theater, which dates back to the 1500s. A Muslim ruler ordered puppeteers to help spread the Islamic religion in Java. The plays are known as the Menak Cycle. In Wayang Golek plays, the puppet master speaks all the roles, sings, narrates, and works the puppets, as well as directing the *gamelan* orchestra.

Make a Menak Rod Puppet

You will need: two .75-inch cardboard tubes, 6 and 2.5 inches long • 2 x 3-inch piece of light cardboard • PVA glue • 6 x 2.75 x 2-inch cardboard box • masking tape • salt dough (see page 5) or modeling clay • four .5-inch dowels, 3 inches long • paints • varnish • .5-inch dowel rod, 19 inches long • short fabric strips • felt • braid • fabric for skirt, 18 x 20 inches • thin string • two plant sticks • beads

1 Wrap and glue light cardboard around the end of the long cardboard tube to form a cuff. Cut a hole in each end of the box. Push the tube through so the cuffed end comes out the top. Glue the tube in place.

2 Squeeze the box to form a body shape. Wrap it with masking tape to maintain the shape. Using dough or modeling clay, mold a head onto the short cardboard tube. Mold hands onto two of the 3-inch dowels. Make small holes in the hands to attach the sticks.

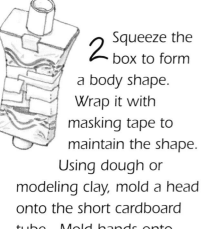

3 When dry, paint and varnish the head and hands. Wrap masking tape around the long dowel until it fits into the head tube. Glue it firmly. Attach the arm pieces to each other and to the body with fabric strips. Glue the strips in place. Make sure the arms can move freely.

4 Cut clothes pieces from felt. Decorate them with braid. Sew the sleeves into tubes. Sew the jacket sides to the back piece. Add the sleeves. Make a long skirt (see page 13), and tie it around the waist. Dress the puppet.

5 Slide the dowel through the body so the neck rests in the cuff. Tie string to the plant sticks, thread it through the hand holes, and knot it. Glue short strings of beads to the ears.

Lifelike Puppets

Japan's *bunraku* puppets, at over one yard tall, are some of the largest in the world. Three people are needed to operate each puppet. One works its head and right arm, one works its left arm, and one works its legs. Handling the head requires the most skill, as the mouth, eyes, and even the eyebrows move. The puppeteers wear black clothes and hoods over their faces so they do not distract the audience. The puppets wear beautiful silk kimonos. Many *bunraku* performances tell stories that were written about 300 years ago. The puppeteers are silent, and a narrator near the stage tells the story. Background music adds to the atmosphere. It is performed on the *shamisen*, a three-stringed instrument like a guitar. The musician, the narrator, and especially the puppeteers must work together as a team. Teamwork is highly valued in traditional Japanese culture.

Make a *Bunraku* Puppet

This is a simplified *bunraku* puppet that can be operated by two or three people. Our puppet does not have legs, but you could have fun figuring out how to make some.

You will need: a balloon ▪ newspaper ▪ modeling clay ▪ white tissue paper ▪ 24 x 2-inch thick cardboard tube ▪ .5 x 2 x 14-inch piece of wood for shoulders ▪ masking tape ▪ corrugated cardboard ▪ PVA glue ▪ paints ▪ varnish ▪ .75 x 4-inch strip of strong cloth, tape, or ribbon ▪ 2 pieces of wood for arms, 1 x .5 x 11 inches ▪ 2 pieces of 6 x 12-inch fabric for sleeves ▪ 10 x 16-inch piece of fabric for undershirt ▪ white paper ▪ 8 x 24-inch piece of fabric for belt ▪ 34 x 60-inch piece of fabric for kimono ▪ 2 24-inch dowels

1 Blow up and tie the balloon. Cover it with several layers of papier-mâché, leaving a hole around the knot. When it is dry, remove the balloon. Mold the face from modeling clay stuck to the head. Cover it with papier-mâché, finishing with a layer of tissue paper.

2 Fix the tube firmly in a vise, and mark a point nearly in the middle. Saw a slot halfway through for the wood shoulders. Lash the shoulders and the tube together with masking tape.

3 Draw around your hand on corrugated cardboard. Cut out four hands from this pattern. Glue the hands together in pairs. Paint and varnish the head, neck, and hands.

4 Pad the shoulders with rolls of newspaper bound with masking tape. Staple a piece of fabric or tape to each shoulder and arm, allowing the arms to move freely. Staple the hands to the arms at an angle. Cover each arm with a fabric sleeve. Glue the sleeves in place.

5 Fold the undershirt fabric over a rectangle of paper. Make a belt in the same way.

6 Make a long T-shaped cut, one yard long and 7 inches wide, up the center of the kimono fabric. Fold back the edges, and sew a wide hem.

7 Put the undershirt and kimono on the puppet, and staple them to the back of the shoulders. Sew the undershirt together in the front and then the kimono. Wrap the belt around the body, and stitch it in back. Put glue on the end of the neck and push it up into the head so it sticks. Attach the dowels to the hands (see page 19).

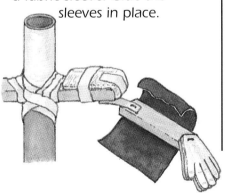

String Puppets

These puppets are the popular Kathputli marionettes of Rajasthan in northern India. They are easy to operate as they have only one string, which runs from the top of the head to the back of the waist. Their heads and bodies are carved from one piece of mango wood, and their arms are made of stuffed cloth. Instead of legs, the women have long skirts that swirl as they dance. Some of the men have skirts, and others have padded trousers that are snug at the ankle.

The puppeteer gives his marionettes high voices by speaking through a special reed known as a *boli*. The plays use many of the same themes as the shadow theater. The Hindu stories *The Mahabharata* and *The Ramayana* are particularly popular. They feature gods and other exciting characters. Audiences love to see the trick puppets, such as the juggler and the horse and rider (page 26). A special favorite is the puppet with two heads, a man's head on one side and a woman's on the other. With a deft twist, the man can change into a woman and vice versa!

Make a Kathputli Marionette

This page shows you how to make a Kathputli puppet head by carving a piece of balsa wood. Balsa is similar to the wood used to make these puppets in India. You may prefer to use another medium, however, such as papier-mâché or modeling clay.

Try making the two-headed puppet using this method. The sari for the woman should cover only half her head and hang down on one side. The man could have a different skirt or trousers on his side. The second string should be fixed on the shoulders to help you swing the puppet around and change its character.

You will need: balsa wood, 2.75 x 2.75 x 7 inches ▪ paints ▪ varnish ▪ two pieces of fabric for arms and headdress, 8 x 10 inches and 2 x 2.75 inches ▪ gold braid ▪ small carpet tacks ▪ cotton fabric for skirt, 16 x 24 inches ▪ two 5.5-inch pieces of braid ▪ sari fabric, 24 x 15 inches ▪ two lengths of light string ▪ braid, beads, sequins

1 Draw the puppet shape on the balsa wood. The body should be slightly smaller than the head. Use one edge as the nose. Grip the piece of wood firmly in a vise and use a craft knife to carve the features. Sand the block smooth, and paint it white and then brown. Paint the features. Varnish.

2 For the arms, fold the fabric in half lengthwise, and cut a hole in the center for the neck. Sew tacking stitches around the edge of the hole.

Roll in the other edges of the fabric, and sew the arms closed.

3 Make a smaller roll for the headdress in the same way. Decorate the arms and headdress with gold braid or ribbon. Push the balsa wood body through the neck hole and attach it at the back with a carpet tack. Tack the headdress to the top of the head.

4 Make a long skirt from cotton fabric (see page 13). Tack the skirt to the body. Tack 5.5-inch pieces of braid in place for shoulder straps. Edge three sides of the sari with gold braid. Tack the sari to the top of the headdress. Drape it around the head and under the arms. Tack it in front.

5 Sew one length of string to both hands, leaving a loop between. Sew a second loop to the top of the head and the middle of the back. Decorate the puppet with nose jewelry and sequins.

Marionettes

This splendid marionette comes from the very strong tradition of string puppets in Burma. In the 1700s, King Bodawpays appointed a Minister for the Theater. Puppet performances became popular, and many plays were developed. They were a mixture of Hindu and Buddhist traditions. The king expected the shows to be educational as well as entertaining. Performances lasted all night, with one play extending over six or seven nights. Some puppets had as many as fifty or sixty strings, with a movable mouth and eyes. The plays were performed on a bamboo stage with curtains behind to hide the puppeteers. The puppets were stored on both sides of the stage — the evil characters on the left and the good ones on the right. This puppet's white face and decorated clothes show him to be a prince regent. Two of these princes appear in the plays, one with a white face and the other with a red face. The prince wears trousers and a *dhoti* (loincloth).

Make a Marionette Prince

1 Form a ball of newspaper around the cardboard tube and tape it in place. Add features with paper and tape. Cover the head with layers of papier-mâché. When dry, paint and varnish the face. Cut a circle of cardboard, pierce a hole in the center, and glue it to the neck.

2 Glue the upper and lower body pieces together in a T shape. Screw an eyelet into the neck. Pierce holes through the upper and lower body with a knitting needle. Make hands and feet from modeling clay. Pierce two small holes in each. Paint and varnish the pieces.

3 Punch a hole in the head with a knitting needle. Make a threading needle from thin wire folded in half. Tie string to a button, thread it through the head, and tie it to the eyelet. Grip each wooden limb firmly in a vise, and drill holes at both ends.

arms

legs

You will need: newspaper ▪ cardboard tube ▪ masking tape ▪ papier-mâché ▪ paints ▪ varnish ▪ cardboard ▪ two pieces of 3 x 5 x 6-inch balsa wood for body ▪ glue ▪ eyelet ▪ knitting needle ▪ modeling clay ▪ thin wire ▪ strong string ▪ button ▪ wood for arms (two .5 x 1 x 2.75-inch pieces and two .5 x 1 x 4-inch pieces) ▪ wood for legs (two .5 x 1 x 4-inch pieces and two .5 x 1 x 6-inch pieces) ▪ colored fabric ▪ felt ▪ narrow scarf ▪ wood for control (one .5 x 1 x 6-inch piece and two .5 x 1 x 3-inch pieces)

4 Tie the hands, arms, and upper body together with string. Do the same with the feet and legs. Measure from hand to hand and from neck to knees. Cut out a simple fabric jacket with a back piece and two front pieces. Sew and hem the edges. Cut collar pieces from felt, and glue them to the jacket.

5 Sew two fabric tubes for trousers. Tack them to the legs. For the *dhoti*, wind the scarf around the puppet's waist and then between his legs. Glue the jacket onto the puppet. Cut a star-shaped hat from felt. Glue it together. Make a small hole in the top of the hat.

6 Make a string control by nailing a short piece of wood to each end of the long piece. Thread the head string through the hole in the hat, and attach it to the button. Glue the hat onto the head. Tie the other strings to the puppet, and tie or loop them around the control as shown. To operate the puppet, hold the control in one hand and the loops in the other.

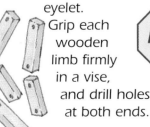

25

Animal String Puppets

Animals are always firm favorites in a puppet play. This lovely elephant comes from India. It is made entirely of wood, with a fabric neck that allows its head to move freely. The string controls are quite simple. The elephant looks very expressive as it walks across the stage and raises its trunk.

The horse and rider appear in the traditional Kathputli play about the Rajput warrior, Amar Singh Rathore (see page 6). He came to visit the court of the Mogul emperor, Shah Jahan, who built the famous Taj Mahal in northern India.

Make a Horse and Rider

You will need: newspaper ▪ three pipe cleaners ▪ masking tape ▪ tissue paper ▪ fabric for horse, 8.25 x 12 inches ▪ cardboard ▪ glue ▪ .75 x 16-inch cord for legs ▪ beads and bells ▪ braid, felt, or ribbon trim ▪ 7 x 1.5-inch ribbon or felt for saddle ▪ 12-inches of colored string ▪ 3 x .5 x .5-inch piece of balsa wood ▪ paints ▪ varnish ▪ felt for jacket, 6 x 1.5 inches ▪ felt for trousers, 3.5 x 2.75 inches

1 Roll and fold a sheet of newspaper.

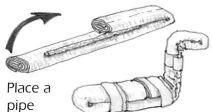

Place a pipe cleaner inside the paper and attach it with masking tape. Bend the paper to form a horse shape. Wrap another piece of folded newspaper around the body and tape it. Repeat with tissue paper.

2 Wrap and sew small pieces of fabric around the nose and rear of the horse. Wind 1-inch strips of fabric around the whole horse. Cut ears from cardboard. Paint them and glue on.

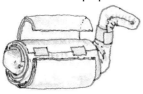

3 Tuck the front leg cord under the fabric. Stitch the back leg cord to the middle of the horse's back. Thread beads and bells onto the legs, and knot the cords. Wrap braid around the body and glue it in place. Attach the saddle by stapling or gluing the ends together under body.

4 Stitch colored string to the head, saddle, and rear, leaving enough for a tail. Wrap and glue braid on the head for a bridle. Use beads, felt, or fabric paint for the eyes.

5 Clamp balsa wood in a vise. Carve the rider's head with a craft knife. Paint and varnish it. Twist a pipe cleaner around the body for arms.

6 Cut out a simple felt jacket, and glue it to the rider. Do the same with the trousers. Tie braid around the jacket. Attach a short pipe-cleaner whip to one hand. Glue the rider to the saddle.

Putting on a Play

In some areas of the world, puppet theater is very complex, involving a whole group of people who operate the puppets, play the music, and narrate the poems and plays. Highly trained people do these jobs, and for them it is a lifetime's work.

On the other hand, most forms of puppet theater are produced quite simply, using very few props and equipment. One puppeteer does everything himself, with great skill.

After making a puppet, you may want to perform for other people. You can do this by setting up a stage that suits your needs and preparing a performance. Before inviting other people to watch, you can practice by operating your puppet in front of a mirror.

Staging a play can involve as many people as you like. You could persuade friends to play the music for you, handle the lighting, design and print the tickets, look after the audience, or make refreshments.

You could also get friends to make other characters and join you. If you are making puppets as part of a school project, get together with everyone and decide on the best play to perform.

Making stages for your puppets

1 Cut three sides of a square from a large cardboard box. Fold and tape the flap down to form a small stage. Cut a door in the side. Pin backcloths to the inside back of the box.

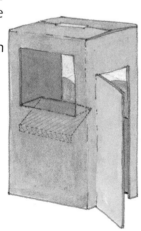

2 Lay a table upside down on the floor. Tape long plant sticks to the two front legs. Stretch a length of fabric between the sticks and another between the back table legs.

A Play Idea For All the Puppets

An emperor has a very beautiful daughter. He wants to find a prince for her to marry. There is no one suitable in his neighbors' kingdoms, so he sends a horseman out into the world to give notice of a competition. Everyone is invited to come and entertain his court. The man who wins will marry the princess.

Suitors come from far and wide. First the princess and her friends entertain them. Then each suitor performs a song, a proverb, a story, a dance, or a fight before the court. The princess gives each suitor a different colored flag to hold.

The emperor cannot choose a winner because they are all so good. He asks the princess to decide. She says she has been so excited by the performances that she has decided to travel the world to see all the countries and their peoples. She jumps onto the elephant's back and rides away while everyone waves their flags and sings and dances.

If you want to make the play longer, you could introduce some trouble. Perhaps an evil sorcerer kidnaps the princess. Then you will have to decide how to defeat the sorcerer and end the play on a happy note.

Glove and rod puppets need a high stage with some form of covering so the puppeteer cannot be seen (see stage 1). String puppets and marionettes should have a low stage so you can manipulate them from above (see stage 2). In India, string-puppet operators often use a sari stretched about one yard above the ground between two poles. Shadow puppets require a special screen (see stage 3 or 4).

3 Using two tables, one upside down on top of the other, stretch a tablecloth across the front at the bottom. Stretch a white sheet across the top. Make sure the sheet is absolutely flat. Fix a small, clip-on reading lamp to a back table leg. Operate the puppets from behind.

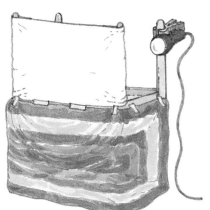

4 Stretch a sheet across a doorway, fixing it with thumbtacks. Stretch a thicker piece of fabric across the lower part of the doorway. Place an adjustable reading lamp to one side so it throws light upwards onto the back of the screen.

Glossary

Aboriginal: having to do with the native peoples of Australia

Amor Singh Rathore: the hero of a traditional Rajasthan play in India

ancestors: people from whom someone is descended, usually family members further back than grandparents

backcloths: painted scenes hung at the back of a stage

balsa: a very soft, light wood from the balsa tree

boli: a bamboo and leather reed through which a man can speak to make his voice sound high-pitched

Buddhist: pertaining to the religion of eastern and southern Asia that is based on the teachings of Gautama Buddha

commedia dell' arte: a style of Italian comic theater that originated in the sixteenth century

dhoti: A cloth garment worn around the waist and between the legs of Hindu men and boys

emigrant: someone who goes to live in another country

fables: short stories that are not based on fact and that sometimes teach a moral lesson

gamelan **orchestra:** an Indonesian instrumental group that plays for religious ceremonies and dramas

Hindu: the main religion of India

Java: an island country in Indonesia

kimono: a long, loose Japanese robe

marionette: a puppet operated from above by strings

medium: material used for artistic or technical work

Mogul: an Indian Muslim who is descended from Mongol, Turkish, or Persian conquerors

prince regent: a prince who acts on behalf of a young king

props: objects used as part of a play or performance

proverb: a wise saying

rickrack: a decorative braided fabric border that is made in a "wave" shape

ruff: a starched frill worn around the neck in some European countries during the sixteenth century

sari: a length of fabric draped around the body, often worn by Hindu women

scimitar: a crescent-shaped sword carried by Muslim soldiers

shamisen: a three-stringed Japanese instrument that is similar to a guitar

sorcerer: a person who makes evil magic

suitors: men who wish to marry a certain woman

Taj Mahal: a tomb in India that was built by the Mogul emperor Shah Jahan to honor his dead wife

transparent: able to be seen through

zanni: traditional clowns in the Italian *commedia dell'arte* theater

More Books to Read

Crafty Puppets. Thomasina Smith (Gareth Stevens)

The Most Excellent Book of How to Be a Puppeteer. Roger Lade (Copper Beech Books)

Paper Masks and Puppets for Stories, Songs, and Plays. Ron Feller, Marsha Feller (Arts Factory)

Puppet Mania: The World's Most Incredible Puppet Making Book Ever. John Kennedy (North Light Books)

Web Sites

Puppet Resource Center
www.legendsandlore.com/puppet-resource.html

Taiwan Glove Puppet Theater
deall.ohio-state.edu/bender.4/perform/pg2puppe/bdx.htm

Making Puppets Come Alive
www.puppetuniverse.com/puppet-alive.php

All about Puppets
family.go.com/crafts/buildmodel/specialfeature/puppets_crafts_sf/

Index